Gotta catch 'em all!

#14 POKÉMON
RED AND BLUE

Over 20 years after the release of *Pokémon Red* and *Blue*, it's easy to see why these brilliant games became so incredibly popular!

Released: 1996
Original Platform: Game Boy
Difficulty: ⊙ ⊙ ○ ○ ○

In the first ever Pokémon games, you control a Pokémon trainer with the goal of becoming champion of the Indigo League in the Kanto region, but you already knew that, right? *Pokémon* has a brilliant mix of collecting, role-playing, battling and exploring. In multi-player, trainers can trade or battle Pokémon, which really expands the game.

Fans went wild for these games when they came out, buying millions of copies, and setting up a franchise that would last for years. You can still get *Pokémon Red* and *Blue* (or the updates *Pokémon FireRed* and *LeafGreen*) on the Nintendo 3DS Virtual Console, and there's also *Pokémon Yellow*, which gives you Pikachu as your starter Pokémon. There are only 150 Pokémon in the game, which might seem a bit measly by current standards, but this is still a stone-cold classic!

Ash Ketchum is one of the most popular and recognisable characters in the Pokémon universe.

Known in Japan as Satoshi, Ash shares his name with Satoshi Tajiri, the creator of Pokémon.

INDEPENDENT AND UNOFFICIAL

THE ULTIMATE

PMON

IER'S GUIDE

THIS IS A CARLTON BOOK

Published in 2019 by Carlton Books Limited, an imprint of the Carlton
Publishing Group, 20 Mortimer Street, London W1T 3JW

A catalogue record for this book is available from the British Library.

The publishers would like to thank the following
sources for their kind permission to reproduce the
pictures in the book: Page 29 (bottom right):
Mark Reinstein/Shutterstock

Every effort has been made to acknowledge correctly
and contact the source and/or copyright holder of
each picture and Carlton Books Limited apologises for
any unintentional errors of omissions, which will be
corrected in future editions of this book.

ISBN: 978 1 78739 289 2

Printed in Dubai

10 9 8 7 6 5 4 3 2 1

Designed and packaged by: Dynamo Limited
Writer: Kevin Pettman
Managing Art Editor: Matt Drew
Editorial Manager: Joff Brown
Production: Nicola Davey

INDEPENDENT AND UNOFFICIAL

THE ULTIMATE POKÉMON

TRAINER'S GUIDE

CARLTON
BOOKS

CONTENTS

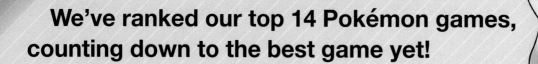

We've ranked our top 14 Pokémon games, counting down to the best game yet!

TRIVIA

In 2009 these games won the Guinness World Record for 'Best Selling RPG on the Gameboy' and 'Best Selling RPG of all time'.

TOP TIP!

No.004

No.007

Choose your starter Pokémon carefully. Charmander has high damage and speed, Bulbasaur has a better defence (but is much slower) and Squirtle is somewhere in between.

POKÉ SECRET

Pokémon stands for *Pocket Monsters*, which was the original name for the game in Japan. At one point it was going to be called *Capsule Monsters* or *CapuMon*. We like *Pokémon* better!

Red Version

Blue Version

Pokémon was first released on the original Game Boy which is why it's in black and white!

#13 POKÉMON
SUN AND MOON

Grab your shades and smother yourself in sunblock because it's time to visit the sunny Alola region!

Released: 2016
Original Platform: 3DS
Difficulty: ◉◉◉◉◉

Pokémon Sun and *Moon* introduced players to the hot Alola region, along with cool new bad guys: Team Skull. Instead of the tried-and-tested formula of presenting a series of gyms, *Pokémon Sun* and *Moon* gave players different tasks such as battles, quests and quizzes, giving the games a light and fun feel.

As you would expect, there's a load of new Pokémon to catch (81 – if you're counting) and there are also Alolan forms of existing Pokémon to collect, plus new Ultra Beasts. Pokémon now have

Rowlet sleeps during the day and battles at night.

Popplio is famous for being a hard working Pokémon!

POKÉ SECRET

Pokémon Sun and *Moon* has a day and night system, which affects the different Pokémon you see in the wild. To track down missing Pokémon, change the clock setting on your 3DS or visit the Altar of the Sunne or the Altar of the Moone. "Float like a Butterfree, and sting like a Beedrill!"

TOP TIP!

Keep your eyes peeled for Zygarde cells! Just like in *Pokémon X* and *Y*, the different cells are hidden all over the region and you'll need to search hard to build your own Zygarde!

new moves called Z-moves, which are super powerful. As with *Pokémon X* and *Y* (see page 28), this game has 3D graphics and all of the characters look spectacular.

The new gameplay makes a welcome diversion from other Pokémon games. The storyline isn't brilliant, and it would be nice to have some more side missions, but this is definitely worth playing. New starters Pokémon Rowlet, Litten and Popplio are cute, and there's a nice feature where you can care for and feed your Pokémon (in case you were worried about them!)

#12 POKÉMON SUPER MYSTERY DUNGEON

Find out what it's like to be a Pokémon as you travel through dungeons!

Released: 2016
Original Platform: 3DS
Difficulty: ⊖ ⊖ ⊖ ⊖ ⊖

What would it be like to wake up one morning and discover you were a Pokémon? In *Pokémon Super Mystery Dungeon* you get to play a human who has been transformed into a Pokémon – how did this happen, and how did you get there? Explore the world with your Pokémon partner to find out!

The core game play involves exploring randomly generated dungeons, which are full of enemy Pokémon, items, treasure and traps. You can recruit teams of Pokémon, so teamwork is key to solving these levels. There are 720 Pokémon ready to be recruited, so there are literally millions of different squad combinations.

(Is it even possible?...
Have I become a Pokémon?!)

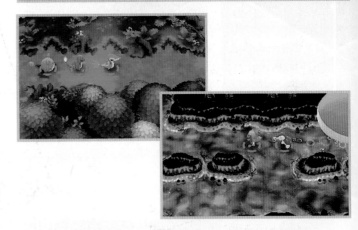

POKÉ SECRET

The story for this game is set in a world where there are no humans. You can take a quiz to find out which Pokémon you will be, or change your answers if you don't like the result.

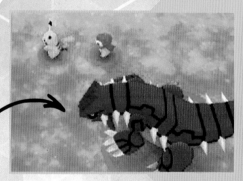

TRIVIA

This game is the first to feature alliances, where all team members warp together to unleash a MASSIVE attack. These linked moves are really powerful!

TOP TIP!

Groudon has the power to disperse rain clouds and make water evaporate with his heat and light!

Enemies only move when you do, so take things nice and slowly to avoid getting overwhelmed. The only way to win a battle is to think ahead. Sometimes it's worth holding back and letting the enemies come to you before you attack them.

Pokémon Mystery Dungeon has a great mix of Pokémon from different generations, all with their own personalities and abilities. You need to move around dungeons quite a bit to work out which strategy works best, so this game might not be for everyone. This is an addictive Pokémon game for players who like to plan ahead.

1F Pikachu Lv. 50 HP 82/82

Pikachu picked up the ◯ Slumber Orb and put it into the Bag.

#11 POKÉMON TCG ONLINE

Play the *Pokémon Trading Card Game* on your computer, phone or tablet – in fact anywhere you can get WiFi!

Released: 2011
Original Platform: Web browser
Difficulty: ⊙ ⊙ ⊙ ⊙ ⊙

The Pokémon collectible card game has been around for just as long as the video games, and has grown and evolved to the point where it's a worldwide sensation! It's a huge game with lots of different and changing rules, so an online version is a good way for newer players to make sense of everything. Players battle Pokémon against each other, while using energy cards, evolutions and trainer cards to give extra power in a fight.

Silvally can adapt its Pokémon-type to confuse its enemies.

Pokémon TCG online is available for desktop computers, phones and tablets, and it does a good job of explaining a complicated game. Some of the rules are confusing at first, so this probably isn't a game for very young players.

This online version is a good simulation of the *Pokémon Trading Card Game*, complete with themed decks of cards, rare cards and different expansions. The game can be a bit daunting because it is so huge, but its size is part of the appeal and makes it lots of fun to master!

TRIVIA

You can use codes from some of the latest Pokémon trading cards to build your decks in *Pokémon TCG Online*.

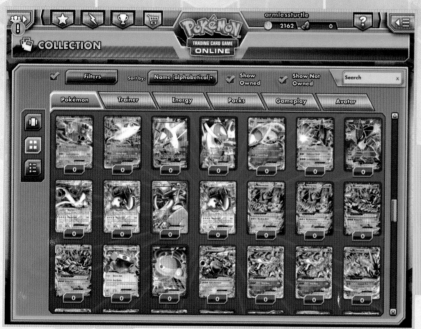

TOP TIP!

Look for trainer challenges and daily challenges to help you build your deck when you first start your game. Theme decks are really useful for spotting any missing any cards.

POKÉ SECRET

If you get good at the online game, then why not think about competing in the real world tournaments? The Pokémon World Championship has over $500,000 in prizes to win!

#10 POKÉMON DIAMOND AND PEARL

The first game for the Nintendo DS lets players connect using WiFi!

Released: 2007
Original Platform: DS
Difficulty: ⊖ ⊖ ⊖ ⊖ ⊖

Pokémon games are always cool when you can share them with other people. *Pokémon Diamond* and *Pearl* were the first games that let players connect using a Nintendo WiFi Connection, letting them battle or trade Pokémon with other Poké-fans all around the world. At the time, this was a pretty big step in the gaming world.

The first Pokémon game for Nintendo DS doesn't upgrade the gameplay

Bonsly looks like it's always crying, but it is actually adjusting its body's fluid levels.

POKÉ SECRET

There was also a game called *My Pokémon Ranch* released for the Nintendo Wii, which allowed players to store and arrange Pokémon from *Diamond* and *Pearl*. The Pokémon could then interact with Mii avatars on the Nintendo Wii.

POKÉMON DIAMOND VERSION

TRIVIA

Pokémon Diamond and *Pearl* were specifically designed to play using the touchscreen of the Nintendo DS. The buttons are colour-coded so they can be used by players who can't read yet.

much, but the graphics are good. Capturing wild Pokémon, battling other trainers and trying to level up as much as possible – these are the classic Pokémon elements that we know and love.

It is one of the best-selling Pokémon games ever created because it just gets everything right. Although the online elements have been discontinued, there is a simple reason it was so popular – it's just really, really fun to play!

Quite a few Pokémon now have more than one ability and learning them all could make the difference during a battle. As always, make sure you know which abilities work best against each other.

The Underground can be found beneath the Sinnoh region in *Pokémon Diamond* and *Pearl*.

Lucas and Dawn explore, dig for treasure and set traps in The Underground.

#09 POKÉMON PINBALL
RUBY & SAPPHIRE

This update for *Pokémon Pinball* lets you play pinball AND catch Pokémon!

Released: 2003
Original Platform: Game Boy Advance
Difficulty: ⊙ ⊙ ⊙ ⊙ ⊙

This is a traditional pinball game where the aim is to keep the ball from falling down the bottom of the table, while scoring as many points as possible. The twist? It's a Pokémon version with bonus games where you can catch different Pokémon by hitting them with the ball.

There are several different modes within the game. Evolution Mode lets you evolve a Pokémon by hitting parts of the board in

POKÉ SECRET

Various rare Pokémon, like Groudon, Kyogre and Rayquaza are hidden in the game. Can you find them?

Kecleon does not evolve into or from any other Pokémon.

TRIVIA

This game was a huge hit when it was first released in 2003 and has sold over one million copies worldwide!

Wailmer loves to play pranks on people by storing up water, then squirting it through its nostrils!

the right order, while Egg Mode features baby Pokémon! The two main pinball tables are based on the *Pokémon Ruby* and *Sapphire* games (see pages 20–21) and they both have similar layouts.

Pokémon Pinball really does feel like a proper game of pinball. The ball moves realistically and the whole game is bright and colourful. There are lots of different modes to master, which should keep Poké-fans busy for a while.

TOP TIP!

Out of the two boards, the *Ruby* board is slightly easier than the *Sapphire* board, so beginners should start with *Ruby* before moving on.

#08 POKÉMON DETECTIVE PIKACHU

Solve big mysteries with the smallest, cutest and yellow-est detective in the world!

Released: 2018
Original Platform: 3DS
Difficulty: ⬡⬡⬡⬡⬡

Detective Pikachu is an adventure game about a Pikachu who teams up with a boy who can understand him. The two must work together to solve crimes in Ryme City, including the mysterious case of the rampaging Pokémon!

This super-cute adventure game looks beautiful and is very playable. Walk around the different scenes looking for clues, interview different Pokémon and humans, and gather information. It's just like being a real detective, apart from the fact it is set in a world full of Pokémon.

This game is great for young players because it's not that difficult. The characters look good and are well-presented. The cut scenes are great and the plot will keep you entertained for hours. This isn't going to take you as long to complete as other Pokémon games, but you'll probably laugh a lot more while you are playing it!

"A bolt of brilliance!"

TRIVIA

The film version of *Detective Pikachu* was being made even before the game was finished. At least, that's what the clues we discovered told us!

Detective Pikachu is a tough talking investigator, who loves drinking coffee.

Turn to page 52 to find out more about the *Detective Pikachu* movie!

TOP TIP!

Make sure you check your in-game notebook to look at all the evidence you've collected. Your case notes keep track of the people and clues that you've seen.

POKÉ SECRET

The Baker Detective Agency in the game is a nod to the fictional detective Sherlock Holmes, who lived at 221B Baker Street.

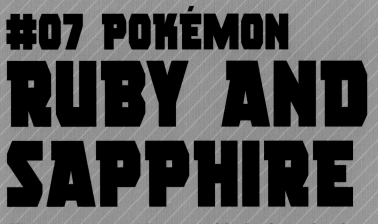

#07 POKÉMON RUBY AND SAPPHIRE

Things start to advance with the introduction of the third generation of Pokémon.

Released: 2003
Original Platform: Game Boy Advance
Difficulty: ⊖⊖⊖⊖⊖

Ruby and *Sapphire* make some important changes from the earlier games, which make everything a little bit easier. Pokémon now have abilities and natures, giving them all different personalities and making the game even more fun to play. There are also new elements, like being able to explore underwater, that open the games out.

Early versions of the games had some connectivity issues when playing multi-player with friends, but updates (including *Pokémon Emerald*, *Pokémon Omega Ruby* and *Alpha Sapphire*) fixed this.

The structure is fairly standard for Pokémon games, but this is a well-crafted and polished game that should be part of any Poké-fan's collection.

TOP TIP!

Many rocks have items on them even though you can't always see them at first. Go up to them and press A to see if there is anything there.

The music for *Pokémon Ruby* and *Sapphire* was so popular that it was actually released as an album.

There is a magnet inside Onix's brain that acts as a compass while it's tunnelling.

Pidgeys have a very strong sense of direction, and can fly back home from any location.

POOCHVENA   LV:2

TORCHIC   LV:5
20/20

What should TORCHIC do?

FIGHT   BAG
POKÉMON RUN

POKÉ SECRET

These are the top-selling games for the Game Boy Advance and you can now get *Pokémon Omega Ruby* and *Alpha Sapphire* on the 3DS.

#06 POKKÉN TOURNAMENT

Gather your favourite Pokémon together, then let them do battle!

Released: 2015
Original Platform: Arcade
Difficulty: ⊙ ⊙ ⊙ ⊙ ⊙

If you're a big fan of Pokémon battles, then this is the game for you. A cross between *Pokémon* and the fighting game *Tekken*, the game is easy for new players to pick up, but it keeps the action and special moves that will satisfy experienced fighting fans.

There are two parts to the game. First, players run around an area in the Field Phase then face each other in 2D combat in the Duel Phase. There are lots of cool moves and different Pokémon to play, but it would have been nice to see more playable characters. *Pokkén Tournament*

POKÉ SECRET

The Nintendo Switch version of the game has several Pokémon that weren't in the Wii U or the arcade versions, including Blastoise, Aegislash and Decidueye.

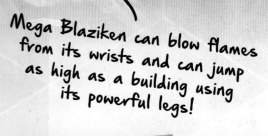

TRIVIA

The game is known as *Pokémon Tekken* in Germany and Austria because both games were made by Bandai Namco. The game uses elements from the *Tekken* series.

Mega Blaziken can blow flames from its wrists and can jump as high as a building using its powerful legs!

doesn't require as much brainpower as other Pokémon games, but it's lots of fun to play! Definitely one for players who think that other Pokémon games don't have enough brawling in them!

TOP TIP!

Remember to dodge and block different attacks and make sure that you use your support Pokémon well.

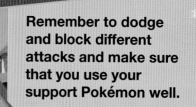

#05 POKÉMON QUEST

An action-adventure game with a fun blocky style and best of all… it's completely free to play!

Released: 2018
Original Platform: Nintendo Switch
Difficulty: ⊖ ⊖ ⊖ ⊖ ⊖

Tumblecube Island is home to the cute, cube-shaped Pokémon called Pokéxel who look a little bit like *Minecraft* characters. Players can create a team of up to three Pokémon to go on adventures and find new treasures.

The aim of the game is to lead expeditions with your team and explore new locations, while battling other Pokémon along the way. There is also a useful 'auto mode' that lets Pokémon control themselves while you sit back and watch.

You can attract more Pokémon by cooking different foods in your camp, which is a really nice touch. *Pokémon Quest* is easy to pick up and fun to play, which makes it great for a casual game. It works well on phones and tablets.

When you enter Tumblecube Island you will have five Pokéxel to choose from: Pikachu, Squirtle, Bulbasaur, Charmander and Eevee.

Be on your guard for plenty of battles along the way.

TRIVIA
The game was originally designed for touchscreen controls, so it's probably easiest to play it on a phone or tablet if you can.

TOP TIP!

Learn to cook well! If you use the right recipe you can tempt rare Pokémon into your camp. Start by luring in fire and grass type Pokémon as they are helpful for early levels.

If you want to lure a Pikachu to your camp, try cooking up his favourite recipes:
- Watt a Risotto
- Yellow Curry
- Milligan Stew

🎮 **No. 001**

Bulbasaur

Seed Pokémon
Grass
Poison

001	002	003	004	005
Bulbasaur	Ivysaur	Venusaur	Charmander	Charmelelon
006	007	008	009	010
Charizard	Squirtle	Wartortle	Blastoise	Caterpie
011	012	013	014	015
Metapod	Butterfree	Weedle	Kakuna	Beedrill

POKÉ SECRET

Pokémon Quest only features Generation 1 Pokémon from the first Pokémon games (*Pokémon Red* and *Blue*), so there are no dark type Pokémon in this game.

#04 POKÉMON
BLACK AND WHITE

Explore the exciting Unova region and train to become the very best Pokémon master!

Released: 2011

Original Platform: DS

Difficulty: ☺ ☺ ☺ ☺ ☺

Genesect is the only Pokémon that can pull off the move Techno Blast!

TOP TIP!

If you want to evolve Eevee into Glaceon then go to the ice covered rock in a cave in Twist Mountain. To evolve Eevee into Leafeon then go to the moss covered rock in Pinwheel Forest.

Pokémon Black and *White* take place in the Unova region, which is based on New York City. There's lots to explore including an airport, amusement park and mountain ranges. A nice new touch is that the seasons change, so leaves turn brown in the autumn and snow appears in winter.

Pokémon Black and *White* don't represent a huge jump forward for Pokémon games, but they are well presented and the new rotation battle system works very nicely. The plot is fun and exciting, with new bad guys Team Plasma providing some really cool moments.

It takes a long time to complete, even by Pokémon game standards, and that is part of the appeal. The massive locations are great to explore, and Unova is a brilliant addition to the Pokémon world.

TRIVIA

Even though some adverts for *Pokémon Black* and *White* featured Pikachu, you can't actually catch a wild Pikachu anywhere in the game! Poor old Pikachu, he probably feels very left out.

Oshawott holds a small shell on its stomach known as a scalchop. It can use it as a weapon or to defend itself.

POKÉ SECRET

There are plenty of awesome side-quests, including one where you can take part in Pokémon musicals! They should've called it *The Greatest Show-kemon…*

#03 POKÉMON
X AND Y

After 12 hand-held Pokémon games in a row, perhaps it's no surprise that for the first 6th Generation Pokémon games, GameFreak decided to add a whole new dimension.

Released: 2013
Original Platform: 3Ds
Pokémon Generation: 6
Difficulty: ☺ ☺ ☺ ☺ ☺

Frogadier can throw bubble-covered pebbles hiting targets up to 100 feet away.

Vivillon's wing pattern depends on the real world location that the game is generated. (There are 20 in total!)

After years of flat, 2D graphics, *Pokémon X & Y* were the first hand held games to go fully 3D! Finally your favourite monsters can be admired from every angle, as you head to the Gallic-themed region of Kalos (see Trivia for more info).

X & Y added 69 new Pokémon to the National Pokédex, as well as the ability to Mega Evolve your pets for the first time. Mega Evolutions are triggered by matching certain Pokémon with specific Mega Stones, allowing them to Mega-Evolve during a fight. If you thought Blatoise was mean before, wait until you see Mega Blastoise's Mega Launcher! There are a lot of great improvements from previous games in the series.

The story gets going much quicker and the 3D battles are truly spectacular. The Pokémon-Amie feature lets you bond with your Pokémon like never before and the French setting gives the whole game a wonderful twist. Très magnifique!

Prepare to Mega Evolve mid-battle and expect awesome results!

TRIVIA

France is famous for many things – from its fine wines and cheeses, to its magnificent châteaux, but... Pokémon? It's true – Kalos, the new region introduced here, is an almost exact match for the northern half of France. Lumiose City, the Paris equivalent, even has a large tower that's quite an Eiffel!

POKÉ SECRET

Ready for a knockout quote? Boxing legend Muhammad Ali once said that he could "Float like a butterfly, and sting like a bee" in the ring, and the quote is referenced in Pokémon's super training mode. Just hit the bags and you'll be told to "float like a Butterfree, and sting like a Beedrill"!

TOP TIP!

I'd like to dine
Tell me more
Another time

Welcome to Restaurant Le Nah.
Our flavours will never overwhelm your palate.

The restaurants in Lumiose City are a great way to grab some easy cash. Equip the Amulet Coin, or some Luck Incense, and then fight the restaurant's Pokémon for some quick money. Level 1 restaurants will give you around P2,000 per battle, plus a bunch of sellable mushrooms. Level 2 restaurants will see you earning between P4-10,000 per fight, plus lots of valuable big mushrooms!

#02 POKÉMON GO

Hunt down Pokémon anywhere in the world in this amazingly addictive augmented reality game!

Released: 2016
Original Platform: iOS, Android
Difficulty: ⊕ ⊕ ⊕ ⊕ ⊕

This free-to-play mobile phone game took the world by storm when it was first released in 2016. Players use their phones to track down and catch Pokémon through a real world map, with the Pokémon then appearing on the phones through AR (augmented reality). The core mechanics of the game are fairly straightforward – catch Pokémon, visit Pokéstops and train in gyms. The main appeal of the game is that it takes place in the real world. You're not exploring a Pokémon region, you're exploring your own neighbourhood!

Pokémon Go works best when it brings people together as part of a Pokémon community. Certain challenges can only be completed by teaming up with other players in the real world. Regular updates, challenges, new Pokémon and community events help to make the slightly repetitive nature of the game more exciting.

Lapras sing at night to call others of their kind.

Lapras are a great choice to defend your gym.

POKÉ SECRET

Some Pokémon are specific to certain parts of the world. So, if you want to catch them all, you'll need to buy quite a lot of plane tickets!

Great Pokéballs give you a better chance to capture Pokémon than the regular red ones.

TRIVIA

There are lots different references to the TV show hidden in *Pokémon Go*. For example, if you change an Eevee's name to Pyro, Sparky or Rainer and evolve it, it will change into a Flareon, Jolteon or Vaporeon, respectively. A nod to the Eevee Brothers on the show!

TOP TIP!

If you want to get Pikachu as your starter Pokémon, ignore the first three Pokémon you see when you start playing. If you ignore Charmander, Bulbasaur and Squirtle four times then Pikachu will appear!

#01 POKÉMON
LET'S GO, PIKACHU AND EEVEE

A game for new players, but detailed enough for long-term Pokémaniacs, too.

Released: 2018
Original Platform: Nintendo Switch
Difficulty: ⊙⊙⊙⊙⊙

How do you create a Pokémon game for new players who have only seen *Pokémon Go* and the *Pokémon* TV series, while still trying to keep long term fans of RPGs happy? Easy – you offer up a big old mix of everything! And it works, most of the time.

The core Pokémon experience is still there – track down and capture Pokémon, train in gyms and battle other trainers. You no longer have to battle Pokémon to add them to your collection, you only have to capture them – an idea taken from *Pokémon Go* that works really well. The mechanics are scaled back and simpler, but the quests feel very similar and are a throwback to earlier Pokémon games Everything about these games is streamlined to make them accessible and easy to pick up.

Your poké partner will stay on your shoulder or your head!

When you're not battling or exploring, try to bond with your partner by petting, feeding and tickling it.

With easy mechanics, this is an awesome game for beginners to master their skills!

Although the games look lovely, they might be too simplistic for hardcore fans. They were designed to be the link between the mobile game and the rest of the Pokémon universe. However, long time Pokémon fans will recognise that it is essentially a remake of *Pokémon Red* and *Blue* presented with 3D graphics.

Your partner can learn special skills that will help in your adventure. They can chop down trees, glide across the sea or take to the skies for a better view.

POKÉBALL PLUS!

At one point the second game was going to be *Pokémon Let's Go Psyduck* instead of *Let's Go Eevee*, but that was abandoned because Psyduck is too similar in colour to Pikachu.

POKÉ SECRET

You can transfer Pokémon from *Pokémon Go* on your mobile phone to your Switch. Just link your accounts and tap the little picture of the Nintendo Switch, then wander over to the Poké Park and you'll be in luck!

Brave the wave with Pikachu!

A female Eevee has a heart shape pattern at the end of her tail.

TOP TIP!

Watch your partner's tail. Pikachu and Eevee's tails start to wag when you get near a hidden item. Press A when the tail is wagging really fast and you'll get a cool secret item.

ASH KETCHUM

Type: Human
Age: 10

WHO IS HE?

Ash Ketchum has one dream – to become a Pokémon master. He hasn't managed it yet, but he will never stop trying! Ash is a ten-year-old boy who has travelled through all the different regions, battling gyms and collecting Pokémon. Ash can be brash and arrogant sometimes, but he has a heart of gold.

Ash changes his outfit when he visits different regions, but he always keeps his trademark baseball cap and Pokéball comb. His best friend is Pikachu, his starter Pokémon, and they go everywhere together.

GREATEST MOMENT

Ash has had too many amazing moments to pick just one. His greatest moment – when he finally becomes a Pokémon master – is yet to come!

Ash is only a nickname. His full name is Ashton Ketchum.

ASH'S PIKACHU

Type: Electric type
Age: Unknown

WHO IS HE?

Pikachu and Ash weren't always friends. When they first met, Pikachu electrocuted Ash and made fun of him for trying to catch a Pidgey! However when Ash protected Pikachu from a flock of Spearow, they became firm friends. They both love battling and adventure, and are fiercely loyal.

Pikachu is just as headstrong as Ash, which is perhaps why they are good friends. Pikachu was given the choice to evolve into a Raichu, but he wants to prove that he can beat stronger Pokémon without evolving. Team Rocket are constantly trying to steal him from Ash.

GREATEST MOMENT

Ash once thought that Pikachu would be happier living with other Pikachu and let him go, but Pikachu chose Ash instead and returned to him. Sweet!

Pikachu is the only electric-type Pokémon that Ash has ever had.

MISTY

Type: Human
Age: 10

WHO IS SHE?

Misty is one of Ash's companions and has been on lots of exciting adventures with Ash, Brock and Pikachu. Misty's sisters run the Cerulean Gym and Misty wants to prove that she is better than them by becoming the greatest water-type Pokémon Trainer. She is super determined, which has helped her to become a skilled fisher and battler.

Misty and Ash met when Pikachu accidentally electrified Misty's bike! Misty told Ash she would not leave him alone until he replaced it and the two soon became firm friends.

GREATEST MOMENT

Misty showed great responsibility by returning to the Cerulean Gym and becoming Gym Leader, even though she wanted to stay with Ash.

Misty was the first main character to own a Generation II Pokémon.

BROCK

Type: Human
Age: 15

WHO IS HE?

Brock was the Gym Leader of Pewter City Gym who decided to join Ash on his journey after Ash defeated him. Brock's time as a Gym Leader means he understands Pokémon battles better than anyone, and he is great at giving advice. He falls in love all the time, but unfortunately things never quite seem to work out for him!

GREATEST MOMENT

Brock once left Ash and Misty to study with Professor Ivy, but he later returned to help Ash win the Orange League Championship.

In his free time, Brock likes to dig for fossils.

PROFESSOR OAK

Type: Human
Age: 50

WHO IS HE?

Ash and his friends need help making sense of the hundreds of different types of Pokémon in the world and Professor Oak is the man to do it. He is one of the leading experts in Pokémon in the world and takes care of any Pokémon that are sent to his lab.

Professor Oak is a friend of Ash's family. Although he is a genius he is quite eccentric – one of his hobbies is composing Pokémon poems!

GREATEST MOMENT

Professor Oak is proud of his grandson, Gary Oak, and wanted him to be successful as a Pokémon trainer. Professor Oak also helped and supported Ash after Gary lost in the tournament.

Professor Oak has his own radio show Pokémon Talk over in Goldenrod City.

GARY OAK

Type: Human
Age: 15

WHO IS HE?

Gary Oak is Professor Oak's grandson and was Ash's rival as a Pokémon trainer. At first Gary was quite arrogant and would tease Ash whenever he had the chance. Gary slowly learned to be more open-minded after losing battles in the Pokémon League.

Eventually Gary decided that he did not want to be a Pokémon trainer and would rather be a Pokémon researcher like his grandfather.

Gary has a group of cheerleaders that follow him around, cheering him on throughout his Pokémon journey.

GREATEST MOMENT

When Ash and Gary finally put aside their differences and became friends. Gary and Ash decided that they are friends until the end! Aww!

TEAM ROCKET TRIO: JESSIE

Type: Humans and Meowth
Age: They won't tell

WHO ARE THEY?

Team Rocket is a large criminal organisation that want to take over the world. They are evil and will do terrible things to get what they want. Ash and his friends mainly run into Jessie, James and Meowth, who are generally quite useless!

Jessie and James team up with a Meowth who is able to talk and be understood by humans. They tend to follow Ash and his team, trying to steal Pikachu whenever they get the chance. They are not exactly criminal masterminds!

Jessie and James were once kicked out of Team Rocket when their membership cards expired!

JAMES AND MEOWTH

GREATEST MOMENT
When Pikachu was challenged by a Raichu in Vermillion Gym, Team Rocket helped him and even cheered him on! What good sports!

Meowth loves collecting round and shiny coins.

Meowth learned to walk and talk like a human to impress a female Meowth named Meowzi... she wasn't impressed.

ORIGINAL SERIES: BEST EPISODES

I CHOOSE YOU!
Episode 1
The first episode of Pokémon has everything; laughter, drama and poor Ash being electrocuted by Pikachu! It's amazing to see how far the show has come since the first time these characters met.

The first season of the Pokémon TV series is sometimes known as *Pokémon Indigo League*. The series follows the adventures of Ash and Pikachu as they travel the Kanto region, trying to win Gym Badges so that they can compete in the Pokémon League. Ash is accompanied by Misty and Brock, while Team Rocket try to stop him and steal Pikachu.

Each episode ends with the Pokérap, a song that raps about all the different Pokémon in the Kanto region. **WARNING:** It's pretty catchy.

THE WATER FLOWERS OF CERULEAN CITY
Episode 7
We learn all about Misty's past when we see her sisters in Cerulean City for the first time. We discover that they are incredible synchronised swimmers and gym leaders.

HERE COMES THE SQUIRTLE SQUAD
Episode 12
This episode has a gang of Squirtles called the Squirtle Squad who wear shades and hang out causing mischief. You really don't need to know any more about this episode because that should be enough to make you watch it!

PIKACHU'S GOODBYE
Episode 40
Can this finally be the end of the road for Ash and Pikachu? Are they going to part ways? Well, no, because there are several hundred more episodes of their adventures, but this is still a great one to watch!

THE BATTLING EEVEE BROTHERS
Season 1, Episode 37
Three brothers are trying to pressure their younger brother into evolving his Eevee into a Jolteon, a Vaporeon or a Flareon. Which one will he choose? This is a must-see episode for any Eevee fans!

POKÉMON: XY BEST EPISODES

Pokémon: XY is one of the best Pokémon series. Ash has new travelling companions – the inventive Clemont, Clemont's little sister Bonnie, and Ash's childhood friend Serena. There's a great storyline about the mysterious Mega Evolution and loads of new Pokémon are introduced, including the cool Zygarde cores. The series takes place in the Kalos Region, which is a bit like France (as long as you don't think about it too much.)

KALOS, WHERE DREAMS AND ADVENTURES BEGIN

Episode 1

Ash and Pikachu are incredibly excited to finally arrive in the Kalos region where they meet Clemont and Bonnie. With a new Pokémon called Froakie to help them, the team are ready for adventure!

LUMIOSE CITY PURSUIT!
Episode 2

A Garchomp has been sent crazy by a Team Rocket mind-control collar and is terrorising the city from the top of Prism Tower. Ash, Pikachu and Froakie have to find a way to stop it!

AWAKENING THE SLEEPING GIANT!
Episode 18

Ash and his friends find a Snorlax that won't wake up! The only way to wake him is to play a Poké Flute that has been stolen by Princess Allie. Ash plays the Princess in a battle for the flute, but if he loses then Allie Keeps Pikachu.

THE CAVE OF MIRRORS
Episode 36

Ash travels to the mirror dimension where he finds out that his mirror reflection needs help finding his own mirror Pikachu. Meanwhile, Clemont, Serena and Bonnie try to find a way to help him escape!

DREAMING A PERFORMER'S DREAM!
Episode 46

Serena's dream of being a great Pokémon performer finally comes true, but will a naughty Pancham ruin the performance for her and everyone else?

POKÉMON: THE FIRST MOVIE

YEAR: 1998

WHAT HAPPENS IN IT?

Team Rocket try to clone the legendary Pokémon Mew, but end up creating a new Pokémon called Mewtwo. Mewtwo isn't happy about being a clone and it decides to take revenge on the world! Mewtwo invites lots of Pokémon trainers to New Island to battle, including Ash, Misty and Brock. New Island is full of Pokémon clones who are much more powerful than the originals. How will Ash and Pikachu ever stop them?

WHICH POKÉMON ARE IN IT?

Pokémon Mew and Mewtwo, as well as Pikachu and Meowth.

WHY IS IT SO COOL?

It's the first ever Pokémon movie! There are three parts to this film; Pikachu's Vacation, Origin of Mewtwo and Mewtwo Strikes Back.

POKÉMON THE MOVIE: I CHOOSE YOU!

YEAR: 2017

WHAT HAPPENS IN IT?

This film is a retelling of the story of how Ash and Pikachu met and how Ash started on his journey as a Pokémon trainer. Ash Ketchum is late to Professor Oak's lab and misses his chance to pick a starter Pokémon. The Bulbasaur, Squirtle and Charmanders have been taken and there's only a feisty Pikachu left! Ash and Pikachu go on a journey, trying to find a legendary Pokémon called a Ho-Oh!

WHICH POKÉMON ARE IN IT?

Well, Pikachu is in it! You'll also see the legendary Pokémon Ho-Oh and Entei, as well as a Lucario.

WHY IS IT SO COOL?

The story of Ash and Pikachu meeting is really cool, and this film looks absolutely beautiful. Plus, the Team Rocket bits are very funny.

POKÉMON THE MOVIE: THE POWER OF US

YEAR: 2018

WHAT HAPPENS IN IT?

This film is the sequel to *Pokémon the Movie: I Choose You*. Ash and Pikachu travel to the mysterious Fula City, for the magical Wind Festival, but what will everyone do when the wind stops? It's up to Ash and his new friends to find out how the city's past can save its future.

WHICH POKÉMON ARE IN IT?

Legendary Pokémon Lugia and Mythical Pokémon Zeraora feature heavily in this movie. Ash only has Pikachu, but there are plenty of classic Pokémon owned by others.

WHY IS IT SO COOL?

Fula City is awesome, and the film looks great. Also the legendary Pokémon battles are amazing!

POKÉMON THE MOVIE:
VOLCANION AND THE MECHANICAL MARVEL

YEAR: 2016

WHAT HAPPENS IN IT?
Ash becomes bound to the Steam Pokémon Volcanion, which isn't great because Volcanion absolutely hates all humans! Ash, Clemont, Bonnie and Serena explore a mechanical kingdom of cogs and gears that has been running for 500 years, looking for clues about the new Pokémon and the mystery that binds them together.

WHICH POKÉMON ARE IN IT?
Loads! Magearna is an artificial Pokémon created a long time ago who is friends with Volcanion.

WHY IS IT COOL?
Volcanion is a fire and water type, making him a steam Pokémon! He can turn water into steam in a second, and fire it with enough pressure to blow away mountains.

POKÉMON: DETECTIVE PIKACHU

WHAT IS IT ABOUT?

Tim Goodman meets a Pikachu that only he can understand, and the two of them team up to find Tim's father, Harry Goodman. Detective Pikachu was Harry's former Pokémon partner, but he went missing after a car crash. Tim and Pikachu search the streets of Ryme City, and soon discover a sinister plot that could threaten the whole Pokémon universe.

This live-action movie is based on the video game of the same name, but the plot is different. There's a world of incredibly detailed Pokémon and the film focusses on how humans and Pokémon can learn to live together.

WHICH POKÉMON ARE IN IT?

Detective Pikachu has all your favourite Pokémon in a live action film. There's a massive Charizard, a cool Jigglypuff and Mr Mime is very funny!

WHY IS IT SO COOL?

It's a live-action Pokémon movie! Plus, every single detective movie should have a wise-cracking Pikachu, right?

IS THAT ASH'S PIKACHU?

Detective Pikachu is a different Pikachu from the one in the Pokémon TV series. There are quite a lot of them around, you know.

HOW CAN PIKACHU TALK?

Only Tim Goodman can understand Pikachu. Everyone else hears "Pika! Pika!" It's cute, but not very helpful if you are a detective trying to solve crimes!

Pokémon	Number	Type I	Type II	Attack	Special Attack	Defence	Special Defence
Bulbasaur	1	Grass	Poison	49	65	49	65
Ivysaur	2	Grass	Poison	62	100	63	80
Venusaur	3	Grass	Poison	82	100	83	100
Charmander	4	Fire	52	60	43	50	
Charmeleon	5	Fire	64	80	58	65	
Charizard	6	Fire	Flying	84	109	78	85
Squirtle	7	Water		48	50	65	64
Wartortle	8	Water		63	65	80	80
Blastoise	9	Water		83	85	100	105
Caterpie	10	Bug		30	20	35	20
Metapod	11	Bug		20	25	55	25
Butterfree	12	Bug	Flying	45	90	50	80
Weedle	13	Bug	Poison	35	20	30	20
Kakuna	14	Bug	Poison	25	25	50	25
Beedrill	15	Bug	Poison	90	45	40	80
Pidgey	16	Normal	Flying	45	35	40	35
Pidgeotto	17	Normal	Flying	60	50	55	50
Pidgeot	18	Normal	Flying	80	70	75	70
Rattata	19	Normal		56	25	35	35
Raticate	20	Normal		81	50	60	70
Spearow	21	Normal	Flying	60	31	30	31
Fearow	22	Normal	Flying	90	61	65	61
Ekans	23	Poison		60	40	44	54
Arbok	24	Poison		95	65	69	79
Pikachu	25	Electric		55	50	40	50
Raichu	26	Electric		90	90	55	80
Sandshrew	27	Ground		75	20	85	30
Sandslash	28	Ground		100	45	110	55
Nidoran ♀	29	Poison		47	40	52	40
Nidorina	30	Poison		62	55	67	55
Nidoqueen	31	Poison	Ground	95	75	87	85
Nidoran ♂	32	Poison		57	40	40	40
Nidorino	33	Poison		72	55	57	55
Nidoking	34	Poison	Ground	92	85	77	75
Clefairy	35	Fairy		45	60	48	65
Clefable	36	Fairy		70	85	73	90
Vulpix	37	Fire		41	50	40	65
Ninetales	38	Fire		76	81	75	100
Jigglypuff	39	Normal	Fairy	45	45	20	25
Wigglytuff	40	Normal	Fairy	70	75	45	50
Zubat	41	Poison	Flying	45	30	35	40
Golbat	42	Poison	Flying	80	65	70	75
Oddish	43	Grass	Poison	50	75	55	65
Gloom	44	Grass	Poison	65	85	70	75
Vileplume	45	Grass	Poison	80	100	85	90
Paras	46	Bug	Grass	70	45	55	55
Parasect	47	Bug	Grass	95	60	80	80
Venonat	48	Bug	Poison	55	40	50	55
Venomoth	49	Bug	Poison	65	90	60	75
Diglett	50	Ground		55	35	25	45
Dugtrio	51	Ground		80	50	50	70
Meowth	52	Normal		45	40	35	40
Persian	53	Normal		70	65	60	65
Psyduck	54	Water		52	65	48	50
Golduck	55	Water		82	95	78	80
Mankey	56	Fighting		80	35	35	45
Primeape	57	Fighting		105	60	60	70
Growlithe	58	Fire		70	70	45	50
Arcanine	59	Fire		110	100	80	80
Poliwag	60	Water		50	40	40	40
Poliwhirl	61	Water		65	50	65	50
Poliwrath	62	Water	Fighting	85	70	95	90
Abra	63	Psychic		20	105	15	55
Kadabra	64	Psychic		35	120	30	70
Alakazam	65	Psychic		50	135	45	85
Machop	66	Fighting		80	35	50	35
Machoke	67	Fighting		100	50	70	60
Machamp	68	Fighting		130	65	80	85
Bellsprout	69	Grass	Poison	75	70	35	30
Weepinbell	70	Grass	Poison	90	85	50	45
Victreebel	71	Grass	Poison	105	100	65	60
Tentacool	72	Water	Poison	40	50	35	100
Tentacruel	73	Water	Poison	70	80	65	120
Geodude	74	Rock	Ground	80	30	100	30
Graveler	75	Rock	Ground	95	45	115	45
Golem	76	Rock	Ground	110	55	130	65
Ponyta	77	Fire		85	65	55	65
Rapidash	78	Fire		100	80	70	80
Slowpoke	79	Water	Psychic	65	40	65	40
Slowbro	80	Water	Psychic	75	100	110	80
Magnemite	81	Electric	Steel	35	95	70	55
Magneton	82	Electric	Steel	60	120	95	70

#004 CHARMANDER

From birth, a Charmander's flame burns on the tip of its tail. The flame reflects their health and emotions. If its flame is burning brightly, it means that the Charmader is happy and healthy. They can be found in hot, mountainous areas.

EVOLUTIONS:

#004 CHARMANDER > #005 CHARMELEON > #006 CHARIZARD

>>>

Pokémon	Number	Type I	Type II	Attack	Special Attack	Defence	Special Defence
Farfetch'd	83	Normal	Flying	65	58	55	62
Doduo	84	Normal	Flying	85	35	45	35
Dodrio	85	Normal	Flying	110	60	70	60
Seel	86	Water		45	45	55	70
Dewgong	87	Water	Ice	70	70	80	95
Grimer	88	Poison		80	40	50	50
Muk	89	Poison		105	65	75	100
Shellder	90	Water		65	45	100	25
Cloyster	91	Water	Ice	90	85	180	45
Gastly	92	Ghost	Poison	35	100	30	35
Haunter	93	Ghost	Poison	50	115	45	55
Gengar	94	Ghost	Poison	65	130	60	75
Onix	95	Rock	Ground	45	30	160	45
Drowzee	96	Psychic		48	43	45	90
Hypno	97	Psychic		73	73	70	115
Krabby	98	Water		105	25	90	25
Kingler	99	Water		130	50	115	50
Voltorb	100	Electric		30	55	50	55
Electrode	101	Electric		50	80	70	80
Exeggcute	102	Grass	Psychic	40	60	80	45
Exeggutor	103	Grass	Psychic	95	125	85	65
Cubone	104	Ground		50	40	95	50
Marowak	105	Ground		80	50	110	80
Hitmonlee	106	Fighting		120	35	53	110
Hitmonchan	107	Fighting		105	35	79	110
Lickitung	108	Normal		55	60	75	75
Koffing	109	Poison		65	60	95	45
Weezing	110	Poison		90	85	120	70
Rhyhorn	111	Ground	Rock	85	30	95	30
Rhydon	112	Ground	Rock	130	45	120	45
Chansey	113	Normal		5	35	5	105
Tangela	114	Grass		55	100	115	40
Kangaskhan	115	Normal		95	40	80	80
Horsea	116	Water		40	70	70	25
Seadra	117	Water		65	95	95	45
Goldeen	118	Water		67	35	60	50
Seaking	119	Water		92	65	65	80
Staryu	120	Water		45	70	55	55
Starmie	121	Water	Psychic	75	100	85	85
Mr. Mime	122	Psychic	Fairy	45	100	65	120
Scyther	123	Bug	Flying	110	55	80	80
Jynx	124	Ice	Psychic	50	115	35	95
Electabuzz	125	Electric		83	95	57	85
Magmar	126	Fire		95	100	57	85
Pinsir	127	Bug		125	55	100	70
Tauros	128	Normal		100	40	95	70
Magikarp	129	Water		10	15	55	20
Gyarados	130	Water	Flying	125	60	79	100
Lapras	131	Water	Ice	85	85	80	95
Ditto	132	Normal		48	48	48	48
Eevee	133	Normal		55	45	50	65
Vaporeon	134	Water		65	110	60	95
Jolteon	135	Electric		65	110	60	95
Flareon	136	Fire		130	95	60	110
Porygon	137	Normal		60	85	70	75
Omanyte	138	Rock	Water	40	90	100	55
Omastar	139	Rock	Water	60	115	125	70
Kabuto	140	Rock	Water	80	55	90	45
Kabutops	141	Rock	Water	115	65	105	70
Aerodactyl	142	Rock	Flying	105	60	65	75
Snorlax	143	Normal		110	65	65	110
Articuno	144	Ice	Flying	85	95	100	125
Zapdos	145	Electric	Flying	90	125	85	90
Moltres	146	Fire	Flying	100	125	90	85
Dratini	147	Dragon		64	50	45	50
Dragonair	148	Dragon		84	70	65	70
Dragonite	149	Dragon	Flying	134	100	95	100
Mewtwo	150	Psychic		110	154	90	90
Mew	151	Psychic		100	100	100	100
Chikorita	152	Grass		49	49	65	65
Bayleef	153	Grass		62	63	80	80
Meganium	154	Grass		82	83	100	100
Cyndaquil	155	Fire		52	60	43	50
Quilava	156	Fire		64	80	58	65
Typhlosion	157	Fire		84	109	78	85
Totodile	158	Water		65	44	64	48
Croconaw	159	Water		80	59	80	63
Feraligatr	160	Water		105	79	100	83
Sentret	161	Normal		46	35	34	45
Furret	162	Normal		76	45	64	55
Hoothoot	163	Normal	Flying	30	36	30	56
Noctowl	164	Normal	Flying	50	76	50	96

#151 MEW

Mew is so rare that only a few people in the world have seen it, perhaps because it only appears to you if you have a pure heart. Mew can use all kinds of techniques, as it is said to contain the genetic codes of all Pokémon.

Mew is so good at making itself invisible, that leading scientists believe it to be extinct or even a mirage that never existed at all!

EVOLUTIONS:

MEW DOES NOT EVOLVE*

*Mewtwo (#150) was created when scientists experimented with Mew's DNA.

Pokémon	Number	Type I	Type II	Attack	Special Attack	Defence	Special Defence	Pokémon	Number	Type I	Type II	Attack	Special Attack	Defence	Special Defence
Ledyba	165	Bug	Flying	20	40	30	80	Dunsparce	206	Normal		70	65	70	65
Ledian	166	Bug	Flying	35	55	50	110	Gligar	207	Ground	Flying	75	35	105	65
Spinarak	167	Bug	Poison	60	40	40	40	Steelix	208	Steel	Ground	85	55	200	65
Ariados	168	Bug	Poison	90	60	70	60	Snubbull	209	Fairy		80	40	50	40
Crobat	169	Poison	Flying	90	70	80	80	Granbull	210	Fairy		120	60	75	60
Chinchou	170	Water	Electric	38	56	38	56	Qwilfish	211	Water	Poison	95	55	75	55
Lanturn	171	Water	Electric	58	76	58	76	Scizor	212	Bug	Steel	130	55	100	80
Pichu	172	Electric		40	35	15	35	Shuckle	213	Bug	Rock	10	10	230	230
Cleffa	173	Fairy		25	45	28	55	Heracross	214	Bug	Fighting	125	40	75	95
Igglybuff	174	Normal	Fairy	30	40	15	20	Sneasel	215	Dark	Ice	95	35	55	75
Togepi	175	Fairy		20	40	65	65	Teddiursa	216	Normal		80	50	50	50
Togetic	176	Fairy	Flying	40	80	85	105	Ursaring	217	Normal		130	75	75	75
Natu	177	Psychic	Flying	50	70	45	45	Slugma	218	Fire		40	70	40	40
Xatu	178	Psychic	Flying	75	95	70	70	Magcargo	219	Fire	Rock	50	80	120	80
Mareep	179	Electric		40	65	40	45	Swinub	220	Ice	Ground	50	30	40	30
Flaaffy	180	Electric		55	80	55	60	Piloswine	221	Ice	Ground	100	60	80	60
Ampharos	181	Electric		75	115	75	90	Corsola	222	Water	Rock	55	65	85	85
Bellossom	182	Grass		80	90	85	100	Remoraid	223	Water		65	65	35	35
Marill	183	Water	Fairy	20	20	50	50	Octillery	224	Water		105	105	75	75
Azumarill	184	Water	Fairy	50	50	80	80	Delibird	225	Ice	Flying	55	65	45	45
Sudowoodo	185	Rock		100	30	115	65	Mantine	226	Water	Flying	40	80	70	140
Politoed	186	Water		75	90	75	100	Skarmory	227	Steel	Flying	80	40	140	70
Hoppip	187	Grass	Flying	35	35	40	55	Houndour	228	Dark	Fire	60	80	30	50
Skiploom	188	Grass	Flying	45	45	50	65	Houndoom	229	Dark	Fire	90	110	50	80
Jumpluff	189	Grass	Flying	55	55	70	85	Kingdra	230	Water	Dragon	95	95	95	95
Aipom	190	Normal		70	40	55	55	Phanpy	231	Ground		60	40	60	40
Sunkern	191	Grass		30	30	30	30	Donphan	232	Ground		120	60	120	60
Sunflora	192	Grass		75	105	55	85	Porygon2	233	Normal		80	105	90	95
Yanma	193	Bug	Flying	65	75	45	45	Stantler	234	Normal		95	85	62	65
Wooper	194	Water	Ground	45	25	45	25	Smeargle	235	Normal		20	20	35	45
Quagsire	195	Water	Ground	85	65	85	65	Tyrogue	236	Fighting		35	35	35	35
Espeon	196	Psychic		65	130	60	95	Hitmontop	237	Fighting		95	35	95	110
Umbreon	197	Dark		65	60	110	130	Smoochum	238	Ice	Psychic	30	85	15	65
Murkrow	198	Dark	Flying	85	85	42	42	Elekid	239	Electric		63	65	37	55
Slowking	199	Water	Psychic	75	100	80	110	Magby	240	Fire		75	70	37	55
Misdreavus	200	Ghost		60	85	60	85	Miltank	241	Normal		80	40	105	70
Unown	201	Psychic		72	72	48	48	Blissey	242	Normal		10	75	10	135
Wobbuffet	202	Psychic		33	33	58	58	Raikou	243	Electric		85	115	75	100
Girafarig	203	Normal	Psychic	80	90	65	65	Entei	244	Fire		115	90	85	75
Pineco	204	Bug		65	35	90	35	Suicune	245	Water		75	90	115	115
Forretress	205	Bug	Steel	90	60	140	60	Larvitar	246	Rock	Ground	64	45	50	50

#179 MAREEP

Mareep has a fluffy wool coat like a sheep. When its wool rubs together, it creates a static electricity charge that lights up the bulb at the tip of its tail. It stores up air in its fur, which keeps it cool in the summer and warm in the winter.

EVOLUTIONS:

#179 MAREEP > **#180 FLAAFFY** > **#181 AMPHAROS**

Pokémon	Number	Type I	Type II	Attack	Special Attack	Defence	Special Defence	Pokémon	Number	Type I	Type II	Attack	Special Attack	Defence	Special Defence
Pupitar	247	Rock	Ground	84	65	70	70	Vigoroth	288	Normal		80	55	80	55
Tyranitar	248	Rock	Dark	134	95	110	100	Slaking	289	Normal		160	95	100	65
Lugia	249	Psychic	Flying	90	90	130	154	Nincada	290	Bug	Ground	45	30	90	30
Ho-oh	250	Fire	Flying	130	110	90	154	Ninjask	291	Bug	Flying	90	50	45	50
Celebi	251	Psychic	Grass	100	100	100	100	Shedinja	292	Bug	Ghost	90	30	45	30
Treecko	252	Grass		45	65	35	55	Whismur	293	Normal		51	51	23	23
Grovyle	253	Grass		65	85	45	65	Loudred	294	Normal		71	71	43	43
Sceptile	254	Grass		85	105	65	85	Exploud	295	Normal		91	91	63	63
Torchic	255	Fire		60	70	40	50	Makuhita	296	Fighting		60	20	30	30
Combusken	256	Fire	Fighting	85	85	60	60	Hariyama	297	Fighting		120	40	60	60
Blaziken	257	Fire	Fighting	120	110	70	70	Azurill	298	Normal	Fairy	20	20	40	40
Mudkip	258	Water		70	50	50	50	Nosepass	299	Rock		45	45	135	90
Marshtomp	259	Water	Ground	85	60	70	70	Skitty	300	Normal		45	35	45	35
Swampert	260	Water	Ground	110	85	90	90	Delcatty	301	Normal		65	55	65	55
Poochyena	261	Dark		55	30	35	30	Sableye	302	Dark	Ghost	75	65	75	65
Mightyena	262	Dark		90	60	70	60	Mawile	303	Steel	Fairy	85	55	85	55
Zigzagoon	263	Normal		30	30	41	41	Aron	304	Steel	Rock	70	40	100	40
Linoone	264	Normal		70	50	61	61	Lairon	305	Steel	Rock	90	50	140	50
Wurmple	265	Bug		45	20	35	30	Aggron	306	Steel	Rock	110	60	180	60
Silcoon	266	Bug		35	25	55	25	Meditite	307	Fighting	Psychic	40	40	55	55
Beautifly	267	Bug	Flying	70	90	50	50	Medicham	308	Fighting	Psychic	60	60	75	75
Cascoon	268	Bug		35	25	55	25	Electrike	309	Electric		45	65	40	40
Dustox	269	Bug	Poison	50	50	70	90	Manectric	310	Electric		75	105	60	60
Lotad	270	Water	Grass	30	40	30	50	Plusle	311	Electric		50	85	40	75
Lombre	271	Water	Grass	50	60	50	70	Minun	312	Electric		40	75	50	85
Ludicolo	272	Water	Grass	70	90	70	100	Volbeat	313	Bug		73	47	55	75
Seedot	273	Grass		40	30	50	30	Illumise	314	Bug		47	73	55	75
Nuzleaf	274	Grass	Dark	70	60	40	40	Roselia	315	Grass	Poison	60	100	45	80
Shiftry	275	Grass	Dark	100	90	60	60	Gulpin	316	Poison		43	43	53	53
Taillow	276	Normal	Flying	55	30	30	30	Swalot	317	Poison		73	73	83	83
Swellow	277	Normal	Flying	85	50	60	50	Carvanha	318	Water	Dark	90	65	20	20
Wingull	278	Water	Flying	30	55	30	30	Sharpedo	319	Water	Dark	120	95	40	40
Pelipper	279	Water	Flying	50	85	100	70	Wailmer	320	Water		70	70	35	35
Ralts	280	Psychic	Fairy	25	45	25	35	Wailord	321	Water		90	90	45	45
Kirlia	281	Psychic	Fairy	35	65	35	55	Numel	322	Fire	Ground	60	65	40	45
Gardevoir	282	Psychic	Fairy	65	125	65	115	Camerupt	323	Fire	Ground	100	105	70	75
Surskit	283	Bug	Water	30	50	32	52	Torkoal	324	Fire		85	85	140	70
Masquerain	284	Bug	Flying	60	80	62	82	Spoink	325	Psychic		25	70	35	80
Shroomish	285	Grass		40	40	60	60	Grumpig	326	Psychic		45	90	65	110
Breloom	286	Grass	Fighting	130	60	80	60	Spinda	327	Normal		60	60	60	60
Slakoth	287	Normal		60	35	60	35	Trapinch	328	Ground		100	45	45	45

#273 SEEDOT

Seedot can attach itself to a tree branch using the top of its head, like an acorn. They absorb water from the trees and the more they drink, the glossier their body becomes. When they stay still they have been mistaken for nuts.

EVOLUTIONS:

#273 SEEDOT > **#274 NUZLEAF** > **#275 SHIFTRY**

Pokémon	Number	Type I	Type II	Attack	Special Attack	Defence	Special Defence	Pokémon	Number	Type I	Type II	Attack	Special Attack	Defence	Special Defence
Vibrava	329	Ground	Dragon	70	50	50	50	Luvdisc	370	Water		30	40	55	65
Flygon	330	Ground	Dragon	100	80	80	80	Bagon	371	Dragon		75	40	60	30
Cacnea	331	Grass		85	85	40	40	Shelgon	372	Dragon		95	60	100	50
Cacturne	332	Grass	Dark	115	115	60	60	Salamence	373	Dragon	Flying	135	110	80	80
Swablu	333	Normal	Flying	40	40	60	75	Beldum	374	Steel	Psychic	55	35	80	60
Altaria	334	Dragon	Flying	70	70	90	105	Metang	375	Steel	Psychic	75	55	100	80
Zangoose	335	Normal		115	60	60	60	Metagross	376	Steel	Psychic	135	95	130	90
Seviper	336	Poison		100	100	60	60	Regirock	377	Rock		100	50	200	100
Lunatone	337	Rock	Psychic	55	95	65	85	Regice	378	Ice		50	100	100	200
Solrock	338	Rock	Psychic	95	55	85	65	Registeel	379	Steel		75	75	150	150
Barboach	339	Water	Ground	48	46	43	41	Latias	380	Dragon	Psychic	80	110	90	130
Whiscash	340	Water	Ground	78	76	73	71	Latios	381	Dragon	Psychic	90	130	80	110
Corphish	341	Water		80	50	65	35	Kyogre	382	Water		100	150	90	140
Crawdaunt	342	Water	Dark	120	90	85	55	Groudon	383	Ground		150	100	140	90
Baltoy	343	Ground	Psychic	40	40	55	70	Rayquaza	384	Dragon	Flying	150	150	90	90
Claydol	344	Ground	Psychic	70	70	105	120	Jirachi	385	Steel	Psychic	100	100	100	100
Lileep	345	Rock	Grass	41	61	77	87	Deoxys (N)	386	Psychic		150	150	50	50
Cradily	346	Rock	Grass	81	81	97	107	Deoxys (A)	386.1	Psychic		180	180	20	20
Anorith	347	Rock	Bug	95	40	50	50	Deoxys (D)	386.2	Psychic		70	70	160	160
Armaldo	348	Rock	Bug	125	70	100	80	Deoxys (S)	386.3	Psychic		95	95	90	90
Feebas	349	Water		15	10	20	55	Turtwig	387	Grass		68	45	64	55
Milotic	350	Water		60	100	79	125	Grotle	388	Grass		89	55	85	65
Castform	351	Normal		70	70	70	70	Torterra	389	Grass	Ground	109	75	105	85
Kecleon	352	Normal		90	60	70	120	Chimchar	390	Fire		58	58	44	44
Shuppet	353	Ghost		75	63	35	33	Monferno	391	Fire	Fighting	78	78	52	52
Banette	354	Ghost		115	83	65	63	Infernape	392	Fire	Fighting	104	104	71	71
Duskull	355	Ghost		40	30	90	90	Piplup	393	Water		51	61	53	56
Dusclops	356	Ghost		70	60	130	130	Prinplup	394	Water		66	81	68	76
Tropius	357	Grass	Flying	68	72	83	87	Empoleon	395	Water	Steel	86	111	88	101
Chimecho	358	Psychic		50	95	70	80	Starly	396	Normal	Flying	55	30	30	30
Absol	359	Dark		130	75	60	60	Staravia	397	Normal	Flying	75	40	50	40
Wynaut	360	Psychic		23	23	48	48	Staraptor	398	Normal	Flying	120	50	70	50
Snorunt	361	Ice		50	50	50	50	Bidoof	399	Normal		45	35	40	40
Glalie	362	Ice		80	80	80	80	Bibarel	400	Normal	Water	85	60	60	71
Spheal	363	Ice	Water	40	55	50	50	Kricketot	401	Bug		25	25	41	41
Sealeo	364	Ice	Water	60	75	70	70	Kricketune	402	Bug		85	55	51	51
Walrein	365	Ice	Water	80	95	90	90	Shinx	403	Electric		65	40	34	34
Clamperl	366	Water		64	74	85	55	Luxio	404	Electric		85	60	49	49
Huntail	367	Water		104	94	105	75	Luxray	405	Electric		120	95	79	79
Gorebyss	368	Water		84	114	105	75	Budew	406	Grass	Poison	30	50	35	70
Relicanth	369	Water	Rock	90	45	130	65	Roserade	407	Grass	Poison	70	125	55	105

#393 PIPLUP

Looking like penguins, Piplup are skilled swimmers that can stay under water for a long time while hunting. They live along the seashore in colder climates and are known to have a difficult time bonding with humans. This means they often refuse food and ignore their trainers.

EVOLUTIONS:

#393 PIPLUP > **#394 PRINPLUP** > **#395 EMPOLEON**

Pokémon	Number	Type I	Type II	Attack	Special Attack	Defence	Special Defence
Cranidos	408	Rock		125	30	40	30
Rampardos	409	Rock		165	65	60	50
Shieldon	410	Rock	Steel	42	42	118	88
Bastiodon	411	Rock	Steel	52	47	168	138
Burmy	412	Bug		29	29	45	45
Wormadam (P)	413	Bug	Grass	59	79	85	105
Wormadam (S)	413.1	Bug	Ground	79	59	105	85
Wormadam (T)	413.2	Bug	Steel	69	69	95	95
Mothim	414	Bug	Flying	94	94	50	50
Combee	415	Bug	Flying	30	30	42	42
Vespiquen	416	Bug	Flying	80	80	102	102
Pachirisu	417	Electric		45	45	70	90
Buizel	418	Water		65	60	35	30
Floatzel	419	Water		105	85	55	50
Cherubi	420	Grass		35	62	45	53
Cherrim	421	Grass		60	87	70	78
Shellos	422	Water		48	57	48	62
Gastrodon	423	Water	Ground	83	92	68	82
Ambipom	424	Normal		100	60	66	66
Drifloon	425	Ghost	Flying	50	60	34	44
Drifblim	426	Ghost	Flying	80	90	44	54
Buneary	427	Normal		66	44	44	56
Lopunny	428	Normal		76	54	84	96
Mismagius	429	Ghost		60	105	60	105
Honchkrow	430	Dark	Flying	125	105	52	52
Glameow	431	Normal		55	42	42	37
Purugly	432	Normal		82	64	64	59
Chingling	433	Psychic		30	65	50	50
Stunky	434	Poison	Dark	63	41	47	41
Skuntank	435	Poison	Dark	93	71	67	61
Bronzor	436	Steel	Psychic	24	24	86	86
Bronzong	437	Steel	Psychic	89	79	116	116
Bonsly	438	Rock		80	10	95	45
Mime Jr.	439	Psychic	Fairy	25	70	45	90
Happiny	440	Normal		5	15	5	65
Chatot	441	Normal	Flying	65	92	45	42
Spiritomb	442	Ghost	Dark	92	92	108	108
Gible	443	Dragon	Ground	70	40	45	45
Gabite	444	Dragon	Ground	90	50	65	55
Garchomp	445	Dragon	Ground	130	80	95	85
Munchlax	446	Normal		85	40	40	85

Pokémon	Number	Type I	Type II	Attack	Special Attack	Defence	Special Defence
Riolu	447	Fighting		70	35	40	40
Lucario	448	Fighting	Steel	110	115	70	70
Hippopotas	449	Ground		72	38	78	42
Hippowdon	450	Ground		112	68	118	72
Skorupi	451	Poison	Bug	50	30	90	55
Drapion	452	Poison	Dark	90	60	110	75
Croagunk	453	Poison	Fighting	61	61	40	40
Toxicroak	454	Poison	Fighting	106	86	65	65
Carnivine	455	Grass		100	90	72	72
Finneon	456	Water		49	49	56	61
Lumineon	457	Water		69	69	76	86
Mantyke	458	Water	Flying	20	60	50	120
Snover	459	Ice	Grass	62	62	50	60
Abomasnow	460	Ice	Grass	92	92	75	85
Weavile	461	Dark	Ice	120	45	65	85
Magnezone	462	Electric	Steel	70	130	115	90
Lickilicky	463	Normal		85	80	95	95
Rhyperior	464	Ground	Rock	140	55	130	55
Tangrowth	465	Grass		100	110	125	50
Electivire	466	Electric		123	95	67	85
Magmortar	467	Fire		95	125	67	95
Togekiss	468	Fairy	Flying	50	120	95	115
Yanmega	469	Bug	Flying	76	116	86	56
Leafeon	470	Grass		110	60	130	65
Glaceon	471	Ice		60	130	110	95
Gliscor	472	Ground	Flying	95	45	125	75
Mamoswine	473	Ice	Ground	130	70	80	60
Porygon-Z	474	Normal		80	135	70	75
Gallade	475	Psychic	Fighting	125	65	65	115
Probopass	476	Rock	Steel	55	75	145	150
Dusknoir	477	Ghost		100	65	135	135
Froslass	478	Ice	Ghost	80	80	70	70
Rotom	479	Electric	Ghost	50	95	77	77
Rotom (Heat)	479.1	Electric	Fire	65	105	107	107
Rotom (Wash)	479.2	Electric	Water	65	105	107	107
Rotom (Frost)	479.3	Electric	Ice	65	105	107	107
Rotom (Spin)	479.4	Electric	Flying	65	105	107	107
Rotom (Cut)	479.5	Electric	Grass	65	105	107	107
Uxie	480	Psychic		75	75	130	130
Mesprit	481	Psychic		105	105	105	105
Azelf	482	Psychic		125	125	70	70

#443 GIBLE

Gible have big mouths, filled with razor sharp teeth. They are great diggers, digging small horizontal holes in cave walls to nest in. They have a dorsal fin on the top of their heads which is strong enough to carry a human.

EVOLUTIONS:

#443 GIBLE > #444 GABITE > #445 GARCHOMP

Pokémon	Number	Type I	Type II	Attack	Special Attack	Defence	Special Defence	Pokémon	Number	Type I	Type II	Attack	Special Attack	Defence	Special Defence
Dialga	483	Steel	Dragon	120	150	120	100	Blitzle	522	Electric		60	50	32	32
Palkia	484	Water	Dragon	120	150	100	120	Zebstrika	523	Electric		100	80	63	63
Heatran	485	Fire	Steel	90	130	106	106	Roggenrola	524	Rock		75	25	85	25
Regigigas	486	Normal		160	80	110	110	Boldore	525	Rock		105	50	105	40
Giratina	487	Ghost	Dragon	100	100	120	120	Gigalith	526	Rock		135	60	130	70
Giratina (O)	487.1	Ghost	Dragon	120	120	100	100	Woobat	527	Psychic	Flying	45	55	43	43
Cresselia	488	Psychic		70	75	120	130	Swoobat	528	Psychic	Flying	57	77	55	55
Phione	489	Water		80	80	80	80	Drilbur	529	Ground		85	30	40	45
Manaphy	490	Water		100	100	100	100	Excadrill	530	Ground	Steel	135	50	60	65
Darkrai	491	Dark		90	135	90	90	Audino	531	Normal		60	60	86	86
Shaymin	492	Grass		100	100	100	100	Timburr	532	Fighting		80	25	55	35
Shaymin (S)	492.1	Grass	Flying	103	120	75	75	Gurdurr	533	Fighting		105	40	85	50
Arceus	493	Normal		120	120	120	120	Conkeldurr	534	Fighting		140	55	95	65
Victini	494	Psychic	Fire	100	100	100	100	Tympole	535	Water		50	50	40	40
Snivy	495	Grass		45	45	55	55	Palpitoad	536	Water	Ground	65	65	55	55
Servine	496	Grass		60	60	75	75	Seismitoad	537	Water	Ground	85	85	75	75
Serperior	497	Grass		75	75	95	95	Throh	538	Fighting		100	30	85	85
Tepig	498	Fire		63	45	45	45	Sawk	539	Fighting		125	30	75	75
Pignite	499	Fire	Fighting	93	70	55	55	Sewaddle	540	Bug	Grass	53	40	70	60
Emboar	500	Fire	Fighting	123	100	65	65	Swadloon	541	Bug	Grass	63	50	90	80
Oshawott	501	Water		55	63	45	45	Leavanny	542	Bug	Grass	103	70	80	70
Dewott	502	Water		75	83	60	60	Venipede	543	Bug	Poison	45	30	59	39
Samurott	503	Water		100	108	85	70	Whirlipede	544	Bug	Poison	55	40	99	79
Patrat	504	Normal		55	35	39	39	Scolipede	545	Bug	Poison	90	55	89	69
Watchog	505	Normal		85	60	69	69	Cottonee	546	Grass	Fairy	27	37	60	50
Lillipup	506	Normal		60	25	45	45	Whimsicott	547	Grass	Fairy	67	77	85	75
Herdier	507	Normal		80	35	65	65	Petilil	548	Grass		35	70	50	50
Stoutland	508	Normal		100	45	90	90	Lilligant	549	Grass		60	110	75	75
Purrloin	509	Dark		50	50	37	37	Basculin	550	Water		92	80	65	55
Liepard	510	Dark		88	88	50	50	Sandile	551	Ground	Dark	72	35	35	35
Pansage	511	Grass		53	53	48	48	Krokorok	552	Ground	Dark	82	45	45	45
Simisage	512	Grass		98	98	63	63	Krookodile	553	Ground	Dark	117	65	70	70
Pansear	513	Fire		53	53	48	48	Darumaka	554	Fire		90	15	45	45
Simisear	514	Fire		98	98	63	63	Darmanitan	555	Fire		140	30	55	55
Panpour	515	Water		53	53	48	48	Darmanitan (Z)	555.1	Fire	Psychic	30	140	105	105
Simipour	516	Water		98	98	63	63	Maractus	556	Grass		86	106	67	67
Munna	517	Psychic		25	67	45	55	Dwebble	557	Bug	Rock	65	35	85	35
Musharna	518	Psychic		55	107	85	95	Crustle	558	Bug	Rock	95	65	125	75
Pidove	519	Normal	Flying	55	36	50	30	Scraggy	559	Dark	Fighting	75	35	70	70
Tranquill	520	Normal	Flying	77	50	62	42	Scrafty	560	Dark	Fighting	90	45	115	115
Unfezant	521	Normal	Flying	105	65	80	55	Sigilyph	561	Psychic	Flying	58	103	80	80

#498 TEPIG

Tepigs can blow fireballs through their snouts. They love roasting berries to eat (even if they do get too excted and burn them sometimes). When a Tepig is hurt it will bellow black smoke instead of flames.

EVOLUTIONS:

#498 TEPIG > **#499 PIGNITE** > **#500 EMBOAR**

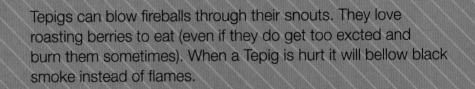

Pokémon	Number	Type I	Type II	Attack	Special Attack	Defence	Special Defence	Pokémon	Number	Type I	Type II	Attack	Special Attack	Defence	Special Defence
Yamask	562	Ghost		30	55	85	65	Eelektrik	603	Electric		85	75	70	70
Cofagrigus	563	Ghost		50	95	145	105	Eelektross	604	Electric		115	105	80	80
Tirtouga	564	Water	Rock	78	53	103	45	Elgyem	605	Psychic		55	85	55	55
Carracosta	565	Water	Rock	108	83	133	65	Beheeyem	606	Psychic		75	125	75	95
Archen	566	Rock	Flying	112	74	45	45	Litwick	607	Ghost	Fire	30	65	55	55
Archeops	567	Rock	Flying	140	112	65	65	Lampent	608	Ghost	Fire	40	95	60	60
Trubbish	568	Poison		50	40	62	62	Chandelure	609	Ghost	Fire	55	145	90	90
Garbodor	569	Poison		95	60	92	82	Axew	610	Dragon		87	30	60	40
Zorua	570	Dark		65	80	40	40	Fraxure	611	Dragon		117	40	70	50
Zoroark	571	Dark		105	120	60	60	Haxorus	612	Dragon		147	60	90	70
Minccino	572	Normal		50	40	40	40	Cubchoo	613	Ice		70	60	40	40
Cinccino	573	Normal		95	65	60	60	Beartic	614	Ice		110	70	80	80
Gothita	574	Psychic		30	55	50	65	Cryogonal	615	Ice		50	95	30	135
Gothorita	575	Psychic		45	75	70	85	Shelmet	616	Bug		40	40	85	65
Gothitelle	576	Psychic		55	95	95	110	Accelgor	617	Bug		70	100	40	60
Solosis	577	Psychic		30	105	40	50	Stunfisk	618	Ground	Electric	66	81	84	99
Duosion	578	Psychic		40	125	50	60	Mienfoo	619	Fighting		85	55	50	50
Reuniclus	579	Psychic		65	125	75	85	Mienshao	620	Fighting		125	95	60	60
Ducklett	580	Water	Flying	44	44	50	50	Druddigon	621	Dragon		120	60	90	90
Swanna	581	Water	Flying	87	87	63	63	Golett	622	Ground	Ghost	74	35	50	50
Vanillite	582	Ice		50	65	50	60	Golurk	623	Ground	Ghost	124	55	80	80
Vanillish	583	Ice		65	80	65	75	Pawniard	624	Dark	Steel	85	40	70	40
Vanilluxe	584	Ice		95	110	85	95	Bisharp	625	Dark	Steel	125	60	100	70
Deerling	585	Normal	Grass	60	40	50	50	Bouffalant	626	Normal		110	40	95	95
Sawsbuck	586	Normal	Grass	100	60	70	70	Rufflet	627	Normal	Flying	83	37	50	50
Emolga	587	Electric	Flying	75	75	60	60	Braviary	628	Normal	Flying	123	57	75	75
Karrablast	588	Bug		75	40	45	45	Vullaby	629	Dark	Flying	55	45	75	65
Escavalier	589	Bug	Steel	135	60	105	105	Mandibuzz	630	Dark	Flying	65	55	105	95
Foongus	590	Grass	Poison	55	55	45	55	Heatmor	631	Fire		97	105	66	66
Amoonguss	591	Grass	Poison	85	85	70	80	Durant	632	Bug	Steel	109	48	112	48
Frillish	592	Water	Ghost	40	65	50	85	Deino	633	Dark	Dragon	65	45	50	50
Jellicent	593	Water	Ghost	60	85	70	105	Zweilous	634	Dark	Dragon	85	65	70	70
Alomomola	594	Water		75	40	80	45	Hydreigon	635	Dark	Dragon	105	125	90	90
Joltik	595	Bug	Electric	47	57	50	50	Larvesta	636	Bug	Fire	85	50	55	55
Galvantula	596	Bug	Electric	77	97	60	60	Volcarona	637	Bug	Fire	60	135	65	105
Ferroseed	597	Grass	Steel	50	24	91	86	Cobalion	638	Steel	Fighting	90	90	129	72
Ferrothorn	598	Grass	Steel	94	54	131	116	Terrakion	639	Rock	Fighting	129	72	90	90
Klink	599	Steel		55	45	70	60	Virizion	640	Grass	Fighting	90	90	72	129
Klang	600	Steel		80	70	95	85	Tornadus	641	Flying		115	125	70	80
Klinklang	601	Steel		100	70	115	85	Thundurus	642	Electric	Flying	115	125	70	80
Tynamo	602	Electric		55	45	40	40	Reshiram	643	Dragon	Fire	120	150	100	120

#610 AXEW

Axew have tusks protruding from the sides of their mouths. These tusks are used for many things, like battling, climbing trees or crushing its favourite berries to eat. The tusks will grow back if they get damaged, making them sharper and stronger than before.

EVOLUTIONS:

#610 AXEW > **#611 FRAXURE** > **#612 HAXORUS**

>>

Pokémon	Number	Type I	Type II	Attack	Special Attack	Defence	Special Defence
Zekrom	644	Dragon	Electric	150	120	120	100
Landorus	645	Ground	Flying	125	115	90	80
Kyurem	646	Dragon	Ice	130	130	90	90
Keldeo	647	Water	Fighting	72	129	90	90
Meloetta (A)	648	Normal	Psychic	77	128	77	128
Meloetta (P)	648.1	Normal	Fighting	128	77	90	77
Genesect	649	Bug	Steel	120	120	95	95
Chespin	650	Grass		61	48	65	45
Quilladin	651	Grass		78	56	95	58
Chesnaught	652	Grass	Fighting	107	74	122	75
Fennekin	653	Fire		45	62	40	60
Braixen	654	Fire		59	90	58	70
Delphox	655	Fire	Psychic	69	114	72	100
Froakie	656	Water		56	62	40	44
Frogadier	657	Water		63	83	52	56
Greninja	658	Water	Dark	95	103	67	71
Bunnelby	659	Normal		36	32	38	36
Diggersby	660	Normal	Ground	56	50	77	77
Fletchling	661	Normal	Flying	50	40	43	38
Fletchinder	662	Fire	Flying	73	56	55	52
Talonflame	663	Fire	Flying	81	74	71	69
Scatterbug	664	Bug		35	27	40	25
Spewpa	665	Bug		22	27	60	30
Vivillon	666	Bug	Flying	52	90	50	50
Litleo	667	Fire	Normal	50	73	58	54
Pyroar	668	Fire	Normal	68	109	72	66
Flabébé	669	Fairy		38	61	39	79
Floette	670	Fairy		45	75	47	98
Florges	671	Fairy		65	112	68	154
Skiddo	672	Grass		65	62	48	57
Gogoat	673	Grass		100	97	62	81
Pancham	674	Fighting		82	46	62	48
Pangoro	675	Fighting	Dark	124	69	78	71
Furfrou	676	Normal		80	65	60	90
Espurr	677	Psychic		48	63	54	60
Meowstic	678	Psychic		48	83	76	81
Honedge	679	Steel	Ghost	80	35	100	37
Doublade	680	Steel	Ghost	110	45	150	49
Aegislash	681	Steel	Ghost	50	50	150	150
Spritzee	682	Fairy		52	63	60	65
Aromatisse	683	Fairy		72	99	72	89
Swirlix	684	Fairy		48	59	66	57

Pokémon	Number	Type I	Type II	Attack	Special Attack	Defence	Special Defence
Slurpuff	685	Fairy		80	85	86	75
Inkay	686	Dark	Psychic	54	37	53	46
Malamar	687	Dark	Psychic	92	68	88	75
Binacle	688	Rock	Water	52	39	67	56
Barbaracle	689	Rock	Water	105	54	115	86
Skrelp	690	Poison	Water	60	60	60	60
Dragalge	691	Poison	Dragon	75	97	90	123
Clauncher	692	Water		53	58	62	63
Clawitzer	693	Water		73	120	88	89
Helioptile	694	Electric	Normal	38	61	33	43
Heliolisk	695	Electric	Normal	55	109	52	94
Tyrunt	696	Rock	Dragon	89	45	77	45
Tyrantrum	697	Rock	Dragon	121	69	119	59
Amaura	698	Rock	Ice	59	67	50	63
Aurorus	699	Rock	Ice	77	99	72	92
Sylveon	700	Fairy		65	110	65	130
Hawlucha	701	Fighting	Flying	92	74	75	63
Dedenne	702	Electric	Fairy	58	81	57	67
Carbink	703	Rock	Fairy	50	50	150	150
Goomy	704	Dragon		50	55	35	75
Sliggoo	705	Dragon		75	83	53	113
Goodra	706	Dragon		100	110	70	150
Klefki	707	Steel	Fairy	80	80	91	87
Phantump	708	Ghost	Grass	70	50	48	60
Trevenant	709	Ghost	Grass	110	65	76	82
Pumpkaboo	710	Ghost	Grass	66	44	70	55
Gourgeist	711	Ghost	Grass	85	58	122	75
Bergmite	712	Ice		69	32	85	35
Avalugg	713	Ice		117	44	184	46
Noibat	714	Flying	Dragon	30	45	35	40
Noivern	715	Flying	Dragon	70	97	80	80
Xerneas	716	Fairy		131	131	95	98
Yveltal	717	Dark	Flying	131	131	95	98
Zygarde	718	Dragon	Ground	100	81	121	95
Diancie	719	Rock	Fairy	100	100	150	150
Hoopa (C)	720	Psychic	Ghost	110	150	60	130
Hoopa (U)	720	Psychic	Dark	160	170	60	130
Volcanion	721	Fire	Water	110	130	120	90
Rowlet	722	Grass	Flying	55	50	55	50
Dartrix	723	Grass	Flying	75	70	75	70
Decidueye	724	Grass	Ghost	107	100	75	100
Litten	725	Fire		65	60	40	40

#656 FROAKIE

Froakie are light, strong and capable of jumping very high up. An observant, but cheerful Pokémon, the Froakie can produce a large mane of delicate bubbles called Frubbles. The Frubbles create a flexible shield that protects the Froakie from damage.

EVOLUTIONS:

#656 FROAKIE > #657 FROGADIER > #658 GRENINJA

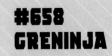

Pokémon	Number	Type I	Type II	Attack	Special Attack	Defence	Special Defence
Torracat	726	Fire		85	80	50	50
Incineroar	727	Fire	Dark	115	80	90	90
Popplio	728	Water		54	66	54	56
Brionne	729	Water		69	91	69	81
Primarina	730	Water	Fairy	74	126	74	116
Pikipek	731	Normal	Flying	75	30	30	30
Trumbeak	732	Normal	Flying	85	40	50	50
Toucannon	733	Normal	Flying	120	75	75	75
Yungoos	734	Normal		70	30	30	30
Gumshoos	735	Normal		110	55	60	60
Grubbin	736	Bug		62	55	45	45
Charjabug	737	Bug	Electric	82	55	95	75
Vikavolt	738	Bug	Electric	70	145	90	75
Crabrawler	739	Fighting		82	42	57	47
Crabominable	740	Fighting	Ice	132	62	77	67
Oricorio	741	Fire	Flying	70	98	70	70
Cutiefly	742	Bug	Fairy	45	55	40	40
Ribombee	743	Bug	Fairy	55	95	60	70
Rockruff	744	Rock		65	30	40	40
Lycanroc	745	Rock		115	55	65	65
Wishiwashi	746	Water		20	25	20	25
Mareanie	747	Poison	Water	53	43	62	52
Toxapex	748	Poison	Water	63	53	152	142
Mudbray	749	Ground		100	45	70	55
Mudsdale	750	Ground		125	55	100	85
Dewpider	751	Water	Bug	40	40	52	72
Araquanid	752	Water	Bug	70	50	92	132
Fomantis	753	Grass		55	50	35	35
Lurantis	754	Grass		105	80	90	90
Morelull	755	Grass	Fairy	35	65	55	75
Shiinotic	756	Grass	Fairy	45	90	80	100
Salandit	757	Poison	Fire	44	71	40	40
Salazzle	758	Poison	Fire	64	111	60	60
Stufful	759	Normal	Fighting	75	45	50	50
Bewear	760	Normal	Fighting	125	55	80	60
Bounsweet	761	Grass		30	30	38	38
Steenee	762	Grass		40	40	48	48
Tsareena	763	Grass		120	50	98	98
Comfey	764	Fairy		52	82	90	110
Oranguru	765	Normal	Psychic	60	90	80	110
Passimian	766	Fighting		120	40	90	60
Wimpod	767	Bug	Water	35	20	40	30

Pokémon	Number	Type I	Type II	Attack	Special Attack	Defence	Special Defence
Golisopod	768	Bug	Water	125	60	140	90
Sandygast	769	Ghost	Ground	55	70	80	45
Palossand	770	Ghost	Ground	75	100	110	75
Pyukumuku	771	Water		60	30	130	130
Type: Null	772	Normal		95	95	95	95
Silvally	773	Normal		95	95	95	95
Minior	774	Rock	Flying	60	60	100	100
Komala	775	Normal		115	75	65	95
Turtonator	776	Fire	Dragon	78	91	135	85
Togedemaru	777	Electric	Steel	98	40	63	73
Mimikyu	778	Ghost	Fairy	90	50	80	105
Bruxish	779	Water	Psychic	105	70	70	70
Drampa	780	Normal	Dragon	60	135	85	91
Dhelmise	781	Ghost	Grass	131	86	100	90
Jangmo-o	782	Dragon		55	45	65	45
Hakamo-o	783	Dragon	Fighting	75	65	90	70
Kommo-o	784	Dragon	Fighting	110	100	125	105
Tapu Koko	785	Electric	Fairy	115	95	85	75
Tapu Lele	786	Psychic	Fairy	85	130	75	115
Tapu Bulu	787	Grass	Fairy	130	85	115	95
Tapu Fini	788	Water	Fairy	75	95	115	130
Cosmog	789	Psychic		29	29	31	31
Cosmoem	790	Psychic		29	29	131	131
Solgaleo	791	Psychic	Steel	137	113	107	89
Lunala	792	Psychic	Ghost	113	137	89	107
Nihilego	793	Rock	Poison	53	127	47	131
Buzzwole	794	Bug	Fighting	139	53	139	53
Pheromosa	795	Bug	Fighting	137	137	37	37
Xurkitree	796	Electric		89	173	71	71
Celesteela	797	Steel	Flying	101	107	103	101
Kartana	798	Grass	Steel	181	59	131	31
Guzzlord	799	Dark	Dragon	101	97	53	53
Necrozma	800	Psychic		107	127	101	89
Magearna	801	Steel	Fairy	95	130	115	115
Marshadow	802	Fighting	Ghost	125	90	80	90
Poipole	803	Poison		73	73	67	67
Naganadel	804	Poison	Dragon	73	127	73	73
Stakataka	805	Rock	Steel	131	53	211	101
Blacephalon	806	Fire	Ghost	127	151	53	79
Zeraora	807	Electric		112	102	75	80
Meltan	808	Steel		65	55	65	35
Melmetal	809	Steel		143	80	143	65

#725 LITTEN

Litten do not like to show emotions. Their fur produces flammable oils, and when they groom themselves the fur collects inside their stomachs which gets ignited and spat out as fireballs. Their fur regrows twice a year.

EVOLUTIONS:

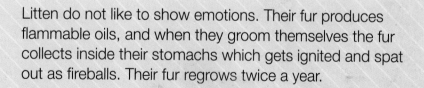

#725
LITTEN > #726
TORRACAT > #727
INCINEROAR